HILARIOUS JOKES

FOR

YEAR OLD KIDS

A Message From the Publisher

Hello! My name is Hayden and I am the owner of Hayden Fox Publishing, the publishing house that brought you this title.

My hope is that you and your young comedian love this book and enjoy every single page. If you do, please think about **giving us your honest feedback via a review on Amazon**. It may only take a moment, but it really does mean the world for small businesses like mine.

Even if you happen to not like this title, please let us know the reason in your review so that we may improve this title for the future and serve you better.

The mission of Hayden Fox is to create premium content for children that will help them increase their confidence and grow their imaginations while having tons of fun along the way.

Without you, however, this would not be possible, so we sincerely thank you for your purchase and for supporting our company mission.

Sincerely,
Hayden Fox

What do vegetarian zombies like to eat?

GRRRRRRAAAAAAIIIIINNSSSS!!!

Why couldn't the motorcycle stand up?

It was two tired!

DID YOU KNOW?

Australia has the most amount of reptiles in the world (over 1000 different species!).

★ There are more stars in space than there are grains of sand on a beach.

I have no blood pumping through me, but I have four fingers and one thumb. What am I?

A glove.

What is as big as an elephant but weighs zero pounds?

An elephant's shadow.

The thirty-three thieves thought that they thrilled the throne throughout Thursday.

Knock Knock!

Who's there?

Broccoli?

Broccoli who?

Broccoli doesn't have a last name, silly.

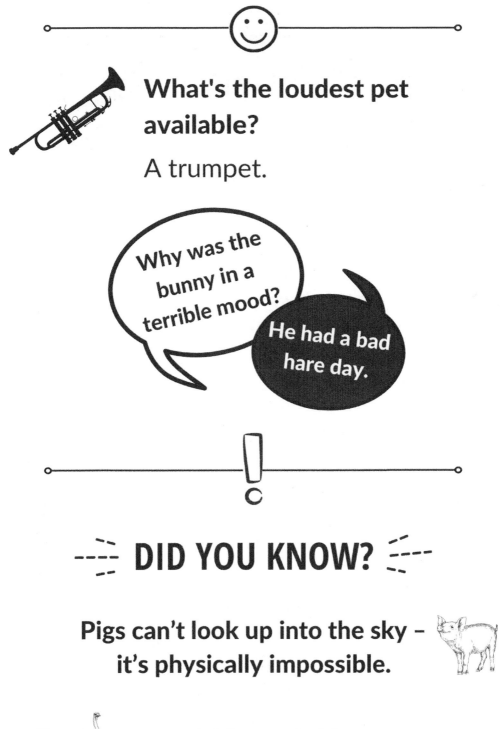

What's the loudest pet available?

A trumpet.

Why was the bunny in a terrible mood?

He had a bad hare day.

⚡ DID YOU KNOW? ⚡

Pigs can't look up into the sky – it's physically impossible.

An ostrich's eye is bigger than its whole brain.

Seth at Sainsbury's sells thick socks.

I come in many different colors and get bigger when I'm full. I will float away if I'm not tied down, and I will make a loud sound if I break in a lull. What am I?

A balloon.

If a white stone was thrown into the Red Sea, what would it become?

Wet.

DID YOU KNOW?

A dog's nose is like a human finger print – unique to its owner.

You can not talk and inhale or exhale at the same time... try it!

Why did the shrimp refuse to share her treasure?

She was being a little shellfish!

What kind of nut does not have a shell?

A doughnut

Who's there?
Wooden shoe.
Wooden shoe who?
Wooden shoe like to hear another joke?

Knock Knock!

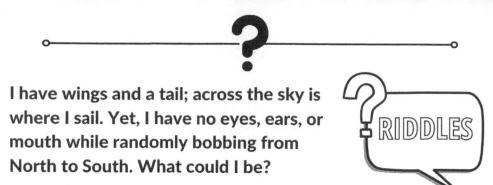

I have wings and a tail; across the sky is where I sail. Yet, I have no eyes, ears, or mouth while randomly bobbing from North to South. What could I be?

A kite.

Make the number one disappear.

Add the letter "G," and it's "gone."

☺

Why did the egg have such a serious face?

He was trying not to crack up!

☺

Who's there?

Amish.

Amish who?

Really? You don't look like a shoe!

What kind of chocolate do astronauts like the most?

Mars.

The difference between broccoli and boogers?

Kids don't eat broccoli!

--- DID YOU KNOW? ---

A pet hamster can run up to 6 miles a night on a wheel.

Monkeys can go bald in old age, just like humans.

Who's there?
Stopwatch.
Stopwatch who?
Stopwatch you're
doing and let me in!

Stupid superstition!

**Can a kangaroo jump
higher than the
Empire State Building?**

Of course! The Empire State
Building can't jump!

What do you call the horse that lives next door?

Your neiggghhhhbor!

Where do baby cows like to eat?

The calf-eteria

DID YOU KNOW?

A group of frogs is called an army.

A bolt of lightning is five times hotter than the surface of the Sun.

? RIDDLES

What do you call a person who doesn't have all of their fingers on one hand?

Normal because all fingers should be on two hands, not one.

When the tide came in, the beach said...?

"Long time, no sea."

TONGUE TWISTER

In Hertford, Hereford and Hampshire, hurricanes hardly ever happen.

Knock Knock!

Who's there?

Lettuce.

Lettuce who?

Lettuce in already!

Why did the pig go into the kitchen?

He felt like bacon (baking)!

Which sort of bugs do the CIA like the most?

Spy-ders

DID YOU KNOW?

The world's tallest man was Robert Wadlow from Michigan, America. He measured 8 feet and 11 inches (272 cm).

What did the potato chip say to the other potato chips?

"Shall we go for a dip?"

Why did the butter decide not to star in the movie?

The roll was not good enough.

Who's there?

Arthur.

Arthur who?

Arthur any more knock knock jokes coming?

Who's there?

Banana.

Banana who?

Bananas not there no more, he split!

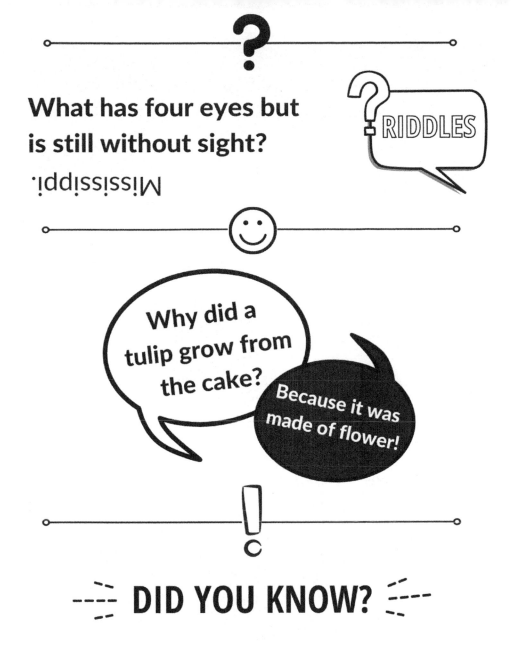

What has four eyes but is still without sight?

Mississippi.

RIDDLES

Why did a tulip grow from the cake?

Because it was made of flower!

DID YOU KNOW?

The human nose can detect over one trillion different scents.

It takes eight minutes and 19 seconds for light to travel from the Sun to Earth.

What do you find at the end of a rainbow?

The letter w.

RIDDLES

What do Vikings like to eat?

Icebergers

**Birdie birdie in the sky
laid a turdie in my eye.
If cows could fly I'd have
a cow pie in my eye.**

TONGUE TWISTER

Knock Knock!

Who's there?
Boo.
Boo who?
Aww, don't cry –
it's just a joke.

There was a fisherman named Fisher who fished for some fish in a fissure.

Who's there?
Fanny.
Fanny who?
Fanny the way you keep saying 'Who's there' every time I knock.

DID YOU KNOW?

Jupiter's Great Red Spot is a storm that has been raging for over 200 years.

What do you say when you lose a Wii game?

I want a Wii-match.

Why do sharks have to swim in saltwater?

Pepper water is irritating!

How does a squid go into battle?

Well-armed.

DID YOU KNOW?

In order to cook an egg on the sidewalk, the sidewalk must be 158°F.

What is the reason that dragons sleep all day?

They hunt knights.

What starts with "P," ends with "E," and contains hundreds of letters inside?

Post Office.

A twister of twists once twisted a twist; A twist that he twisted was a three-twisted twist; If in twisting a twist one twist should untwist, The untwisted twist would untwist the twist.

Knock Knock!

Who's there?

Police.

Police who?

Let me in? Police and thank you!

What did the horse say when it fell?

I've fallen and I can't giddyup!

What did one firefly say to the other?

You glow girl!

DID YOU KNOW?

The biggest pizza ever created was 13,580 square feet, made in Rome, Italy.

I am a word. If you pronounce
me right, you are wrong;
if you pronounce me wrong,
you are right. What word am I?

Wrong.

What do an island and the letter
"T" have in common?

They are both in the middle of "water."

Tom threw Tim three thumbtacks.

TONGUE TWISTER

Red Buick, blue Buick

Knock
Knock!

Who's there?
Those.
Those who?
Those knock-knock
jokes were great!

What do you call a reindeer with bad manners?

Rude-olph

Why did the Christmas tree go to the barber?

It needed to be trimmed.

Who's there?

Nicholas

Nicholas who?

Nicholas half as much as a dime!

Who's there?

Yoda.

Yoda who?

Yoda leh ee-hoo!

DID YOU KNOW?

The artists who voiced Mickey Mouse & Minnie Mouse were married in real life.

The first organized baseball game was played in New Jersey in 1846.

A cat snaps a rat's paxwax.

TONGUE TWISTER

Knock Knock!

Who's there?

Argue.

Argue who?

Argue going to let me in?

Why did the policeman go to the baseball game?

He heard someone stole a base!

DID YOU KNOW?

Green eyes are more common in females than males.

If you notice this notice,
you will notice that this notice
is not worth noticing.

TONGUE TWISTER

A gazillion gigantic grapes gushed
gradually giving gophers gooey guts.

Who's there?

Dozen.

Dozen who?

Dozen anyone want to
let me in!

Knock
Knock!

What is a waiter's favorite sport?

Tennis, because they know how to serve.

DID YOU KNOW?

Greenland sharks can live up to 500 years!

If you understand,
say "understand".
If you don't understand,
say "don't understand".

TONGUE TWISTER

Knock Knock!

Who's there?

Eva.

Eva who?

Eva I told you, would you let me in?

How do trees access the internet?

By logging in

What lies at the bottom of the ocean, worrying?

A nervous wreck.

When will the little snake arrive?

I don't know, but she won't be long.

Who's there?
Harriet.
Harriet who?
Harriet it up,
it's cold out here!

DID YOU KNOW?

There are 162 stairs inside the Statue of Liberty, from the bottom to the top of her head.

Two to two to Toulouse?

Linda-Lou Lambert loves lemon lollipop lipgloss.

Who's there?
Hugh.
Hugh who?
Hugh is going to let me in then?

Why did Dracula lie in the wrong coffin?

He made a grave mistake.

Why should you not let a bear operate the remote?

He will keep pressing the PAWS button.

Who's there?
Ken.
Ken who?
Ken I come in or do I have to climb through a window!

Knock Knock!

Who's there?
Aaron.
Aaron who?
Why Aaron you opening the door?

Knock Knock!

DID YOU KNOW?

The 7 layers of rings around Saturn are made up of ice crystals! Some of the crystals are as big as a house and some are as small as a speck of dust.

Near an ear, a nearer ear,
a nearly eerie ear

Which wristwatches are
Swiss wristwatches?

Who's there?
Abbott.
Abbott who?
Abbott time you
answered the door!

Why did the laptop get glasses?

To improve its web sight.

Why were the cornflakes scared of the woman?

Because she was a cereal killer!

Where do crayons go on holiday?

Color-ado

Any noise annoys an oyster, but a noisy noise annoys an oyster more.

TONGUE TWISTER

Knock Knock!

Who's there?
Adore.
Adore who?
Adore is between you and me!

What do you call a sick eagle!

Ill-eagle!

What did the painter say to the wall?

One more crack like that and I'll plaster you!

DID YOU KNOW?

The distance from your inner elbow to your wrist is the same as the length of your foot.

About 50% of the dust in your house is made up of dead skin.

Rubber baby buggy bumpers.

TONGUE TWISTER

Red lorry, yellow lorry.

Knock Knock!

Who's there?

Cher.

Cher who?

Cher would be nice if you opened the door!

Why can't you borrow money from a leprechaun?

Because they're always a little short!

Are any Halloween monsters good at math?

No, unless you Count Dracula!

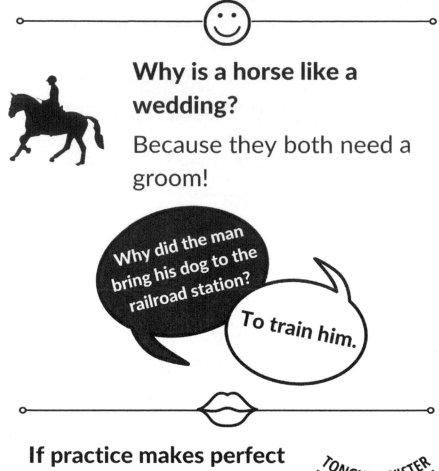

Why is a horse like a wedding?

Because they both need a groom!

Why did the man bring his dog to the railroad station?

To train him.

If practice makes perfect and perfect needs practice, I'm perfectly practiced and practically perfect.

TONGUE TWISTER

Knock Knock!

Who's there?
Doris.
Doris who?
Doris locked, I'm coming in through the window!

What season is it when you are on a trampoline?

Spring time.

Why did the tortilla chip start dancing?

Because they put on the salsa.

! DID YOU KNOW?

Rabbits and parrots can see behind themselves without even moving their heads!

Send the tense toast to the ten tall tents.

TONGUE TWISTER

Who's there?
Howl.
Howl who?
Howl you know it's really me unless you open the door?

Knock Knock!

Why did the jellybean go to school?

To become a smartie!

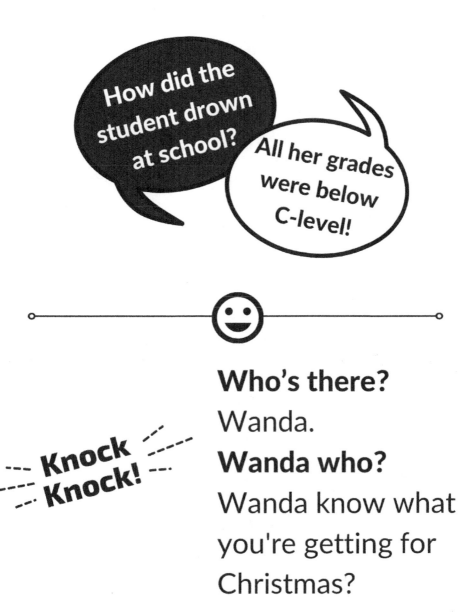

How did the student drown at school?

All her grades were below C-level!

Knock Knock!

Who's there?
Wanda.
Wanda who?
Wanda know what you're getting for Christmas?

❗ DID YOU KNOW?

In France, a "crepe" is just a really  thin pancake.

Mrs. Hunt had a country cut front in the front of her country cut petty coat.

TONGUE TWISTER

Knock Knock!

Who's there?

Olive.

Olive who?

Olive right next door to you.

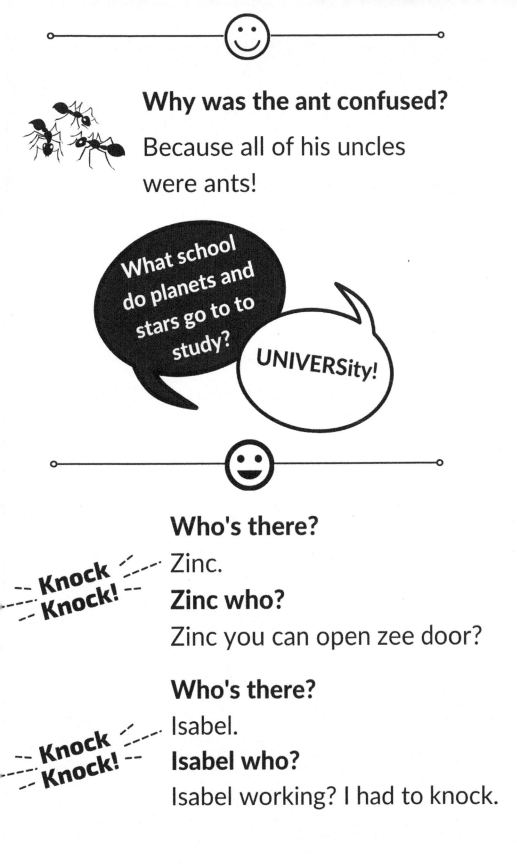

Why was the ant confused?

Because all of his uncles were ants!

What school do planets and stars go to to study?

UNIVERSity!

Who's there?

Knock Knock!

Zinc.

Zinc who?

Zinc you can open zee door?

Who's there?

Knock Knock!

Isabel.

Isabel who?

Isabel working? I had to knock.

DID YOU KNOW?

Alpacas are known to spit when they get annoyed.

It took one and half years to build Cinderella's castle in Disney World.

Who's there?

Yule.

Yule who?

Yule never know if you don't answer the door!

There's a sandwich on the sand which was sent by a sane witch.

Where do dogs go when they lose their tail?

To the retail store.

Why couldn't the cat play games on the computer?

Because she ate the mouse.

Who's there?
Carrie.
Carrie who?
Carrie me home, my feet are tired!

Knock Knock!

Who's there?
Toot.
Toot who?
Toot the bitter end!

Knock Knock!

DID YOU KNOW?

There may be aliens in our solar system. However, they are likely to be bacteria or microbes.

10% of the bones in a cat are located in its tail.

Who's there?
Justin.
Justin who?
Justin time! I thought you weren't home.

Knock Knock!

A box of biscuits, a box of mixed biscuits, and a biscuit mixer.

TONGUE TWISTER

What do you call two spiders who got married?

Newlyweb!

What do you think about eating clocks?

It is a waste of time.

❗

--- DID YOU KNOW? ---

Fortune cookies are an American thing—it was invented by someone in San Francisco in 1890.

Only 3% of Earth's water is freshwater. The rest is saltwater.

Who's there?

Chicken.

Knock Knock!

Chicken who?

Chicken your pockets.

I think your keys are there!

Tim, the thin twin tinsmith.

TONGUE TWISTER

Who's there?
Handsome.
Handsome who?
Handsome chips through the keyhole and I'll tell you more!

Who's there?
Juno.
Juno who?
Juno how long I've been knocking on this door?

Mr. Fister's sister sold sea shells by the sea shore. Mr. Fister didn't sell sea shells, he sold silk sheets

TONGUE TWISTER

Why was the baby strawberry crying?

Because her parents were in a jam.

How are false teeth like stars?

They come out at night!

Who's there?
Butter.
Butter who?
Butter open quick, I have a funny Halloween joke to tell you!

Knock Knock!

Who's there?
Sacha.
Sacha who?
Sacha fuss, just because
I knocked on your door.

Who's there?
Leena.
Leena who?
Leena little closer and
I will tell you.

King Thistle stuck a thousand thistles in the thistle of his thumb.

What do you call a dog magician?

A labracadabrador.

Where do pencils go on vacation?

Pencil-vania.

Who's there?
Ohio.
Ohio who?
Ohio feeling?

Who's there?
Abby and Manny.
Abby and Manny who?
Abby birthday and
Manny happy returns.

**Did Dick Pickens prick
his pinkie pickling cheap cling
peaches in an inch of
Pinch or framing his famed
French finch photos?**

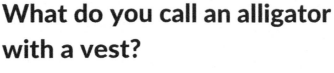

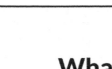

What do you call an alligator with a vest?

An investigator!

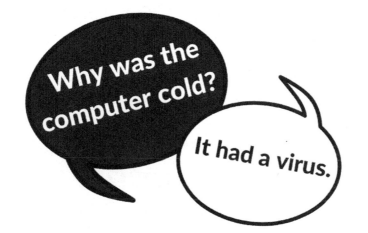

Why was the computer cold?

It had a virus.

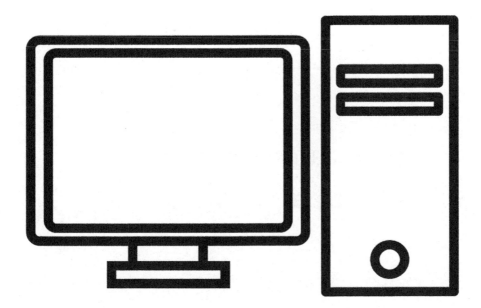

Knock Knock!

Who's there?
William.
William who?
William be my Valentine?

Knock Knock!

Who's there?
Annie.
Annie who?
Annie-versary!

TONGUE TWISTER

**How many berries
could a bare berry carry,
if a bare berry
could carry berries?**

How do pickles enjoy a day out?

They relish it.

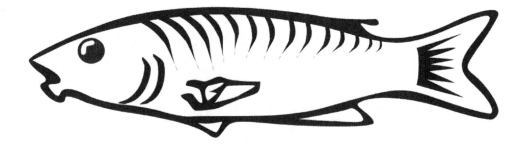

Who's there?
Cash.
Cash who?
You're nuts!

Who's there?
Mark.
Mark who?
Mark your calendars.
My birthday's just
around the corner!

**Ned Nott was shot
and Sam Shott was
not, so is it better to
be Shott than Nott?**

TONGUE TWISTER

How do you throw a party in space?

You planet.

Why are robots never afraid?

They have nerves of steel.

Who's there?
Doughnut.
Doughnut who?
Doughnut worry it is just a knock knock joke!

Who's there?
Vampire.
Vampire who?
Vampire state building!

The owner of the inside inn was inside his inside inn with his inside outside his inside inn.

What do you get when you cross a centipede with a parrot?

A walkie talkie.

What does bread do on vacation?

Loaf around.

Who's there?
Matty.
Matty who?
Matty nice of you to invite me to the party!

Who's there?

Dewey.

Dewey who?

Dewey have to wait long to eat?

Who's there?

Wilma.

Wilma who?

Wil Ma make lots of food again this Thanksgiving?

Peter Piper picked a peck of pickled peppers.

TONGUE TWISTER

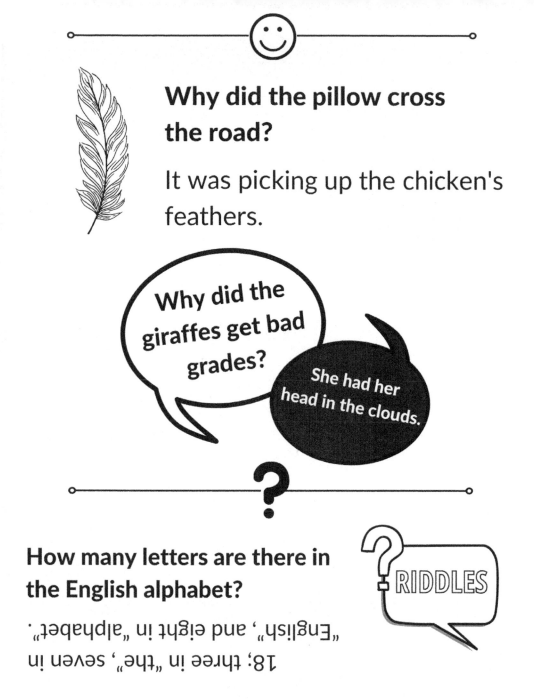

Why did the pillow cross the road?

It was picking up the chicken's feathers.

Why did the giraffes get bad grades?

She had her head in the clouds.

How many letters are there in the English alphabet?

18; three in "the", seven in "English", and eight in "alphabet".

A doctor and a boy were walking. The boy was the doctor's son, but the doctor was not the boy's father. Who was the doctor?

His mother.

Who's there?
Iowa.
Iowa who?
Iowa you a dollar!

Who's there?
Gorilla.
Gorilla who?
Gorilla me a steak.

**The seven silly sheep
Silly Sally shooed
Shilly-shallied south.**

Willie's really weary.

What is a scarecrow's favorite fruit?

A strawberry.

Why did the king go to the bathroom?

He wanted to sit on the throne.

A monkey, a squirrel, and a bird are racing to the top of a coconut tree. Who will get the banana first?

RIDDLES

None of them because a banana can't grow from a coconut tree.

A man in a car saw a Golden Door, Silver Door, and a Bronze Door. Which door did he open first?

The car door.

Who's there?

Cow.

Cow who?

Cow much longer are you going to put up with all this knocking?

Who's there?

Cowsgo.

Cowsgo who?

No they don't, cows-go moo.

Betty Botter bought some butter but she said the butter's bitter.

TONGUE TWISTER

Mary Mac's mother's making Mary Mac marry me.

What does a broken plate say when she gets her cupcake?

Is this GLUE-ten free?

Why do hockey players make great bankers?

Because they are good at checking.

On a horse, Scott rode into town on Friday. He stayed for two days and then left on Friday. How is this possible?

RIDDLES

Friday is the name of his horse.

Its mother is a cloud, its father is the wind, its son is a stream, and its daughter is land. What is it?

Rain.

What instrument can you hear but never see?

Your voice. You can sing (instrument) and hear it but can never see it.

RIDDLES

What is as light as a feather, but not even the world's strongest man can hold it for longer than five minutes?

Breath.

I know a boy named Tate who dined with his girl at eight eight.

TONGUE TWISTER

Knock Knock!

Who's there?

Bert.

Bert who?

Bert the toast, try again.

Why was the snowman at the grocery store?

Because he was picking his nose.

How did the baby tell her mom she had a wet diaper?

She sent her a pee-mail.

?

As a man walked across a bridge, he found wood that was neither straight nor crooked. What kind of wood was it?

Sawdust.

RIDDLES

Tuesday, Sam and Peter went out to lunch. After they ate, they paid the bill, but Sam and Peter didn't pay. How is this possible?

Tuesday paid; it's one of their friends.

Knock Knock!

Who's there?
Peg.
Peg who?
Peg your pardon—I've got the wrong door.

What kind of vegetable is angry?

A steamed carrot!

TONGUE TWISTER

She sells seashells on the seashore. The shells she sells are seashells, I'm sure.

What do you do when an astronaut's wife is upset?

Give her some space.

What do you call a deer with no eyes?

(in a southern accent) "I got no eye-deer!"

The farther you take me, the more of me you leave behind. What am I?

Footsteps.

How is Europe like a frying pan?

Because it has Greece at the bottom.

What has a head that never weeps, a bed that never sleeps, can run but cannot walk, and has a bank but no money?

RIDDLES

A river.

The one who made me does not need me; the one who buys me does not use me; the one who uses me does not know. What am I?

Coffin.

Who's there?

Clear.

Clear who?

Clear this hallway for delivery.

Knock Knock!

Pad kid poured curd pulled cod.

TONGUE TWISTER

How do you get a cat to code?

You Scratch it!

What did the fisherman say to the magician?

"Pick a cod, any cod."

What do you call a retired vegetable?

A has-bean.

You throw me away when you need me and bring me back when I'm not needed. What am I?

An anchor.

RIDDLES

It gets beaten and whipped without ever shedding a tear. What is it?

An egg.

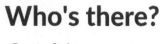

Who's there?
Cookie.
Cookie who?
Cookie quit and now I
have to make all the food!

Who's there?
Dee.
Dee who?
Dee-licious!

I like New York,
unique New York, I like
unique New York.

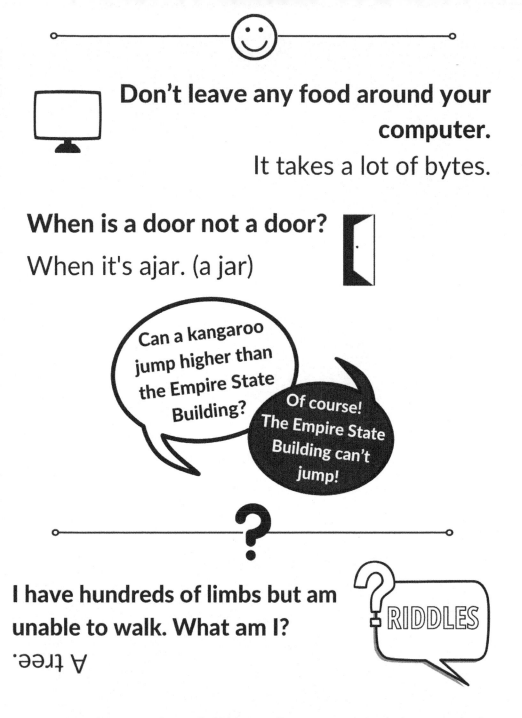

Don't leave any food around your computer.

It takes a lot of bytes.

When is a door not a door?

When it's ajar. (a jar)

Can a kangaroo jump higher than the Empire State Building?

Of course! The Empire State Building can't jump!

I have hundreds of limbs but am unable to walk. What am I?

A tree.

RIDDLES

Using only addition, how can you use eight eights to get the number 1,000?

8+8+8+88+888

Who's there?
Ketchup.
Ketchup who?
Ketchup with me and
I'll tell you!

Who's there?
Oswald.
Oswald who?
Oswald my gum.

Through three cheese trees
three free fleas flew.
While these fleas flew,
freezy breeze blew.
Freezy breeze made
these three trees freeze.
Freezy trees made
these trees' cheese freeze.
That's what made
these three free fleas sneeze.

I spent five minutes fixing a broken clock yesterday...

At least, I think it was five minutes...

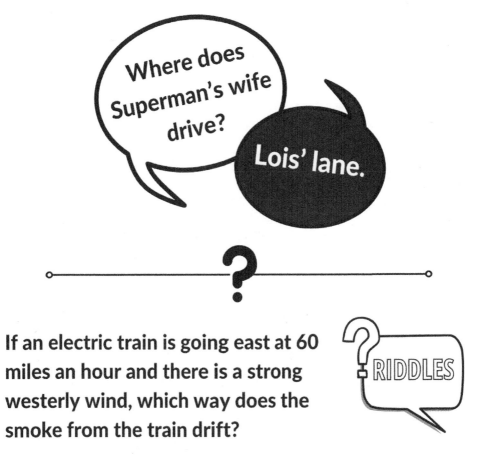

If an electric train is going east at 60 miles an hour and there is a strong westerly wind, which way does the smoke from the train drift?

There is no smoke coming from electric trains.

I shave every day but my beard never changes. What am I?

A barber.

Who's there?
Bernadette.
Bernadette who?
Bernadette ate all my dinner and now I'm starving!

Who's there?
Eaton
Eaton who?
Eaton cookies, need some milk.

She had shoulder surgery.

Ah shucks, six stick shifts stuck shut!

Why did the garden feel overcrowded?

There wasn't mushroom.

Why did Mom hit the cake with a hammer?

It was a pound cake.

They come out at night without being called and are lost in the day without being stolen. What are they?

RIDDLES

The stars.

I have branches but no fruit, trunk, or leaves. What am I?

A bank.

Who's there?

I scream.

I scream who?

I scream tastes cool on a hot day.

Who's there?

Ice Cream.

Ice Cream who?

I scream so you'll open the door.

Mary Mac's mother's making Mary Mac marry me.
My mother's making me marry Mary Mac.

TONGUE TWISTER

What do you call a hen who counts her eggs?

A mathemachicken.

Did you hear the joke about the germ?

Actually, never mind. Can't spread it around!

What can't be put in a saucepan?

Its lid.

RIDDLES

Forward I am heavy but backward I am not. What am I?

The word "ton".

Who's there?
Ada.
Ada who?
Ada burger for lunch!

Who's there?
Organ.
Organ who?
Organ-ize a party, it's my birthday!

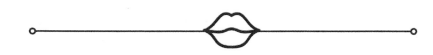

**Betty Botter
bought some butter but
she said the butter's bitter.
If I put it in my batter it will
make my batter bitter.**

What kind of dog does Dracula have?

A bloodhound!

What do you say when you catch a ghost?

"Gotchu Boo!"

What five-letter word has one left when two are removed?

Stone.

RIDDLES

What has many needles but doesn't sew?

A Christmas tree.

--- DID YOU KNOW? ---

You might consider New York City or Los Angeles to be the largest city in North America. However, Mexico City is actually the largest!

Knock Knock!

Who's there?
Philip
Philip who?
Philip the car,
we're out of gas.

Knock Knock!

Who's there?
Hada
Hada who?
Had a great time,
how about you?

**How much dough
would Bob Dole dole
if Bob Dole could dole dough?**

TONGUE TWISTER

**Rattle your bottles
in Rollocks' van.**

If athletes get athlete's foot, then what do astronauts get?
Missle-toe.

Sometimes I tuck my knees into my chest and lean forward.

That's just how I roll.

I have one eye but am unable to see. What am I?
A needle.

RIDDLES

Ravens can learn how to speak better than parrots.

Tie a knot, tie a knot.
Tie a tight, tight knot.
Tie a knot in the shape
of a naught.

Who's there?
Shh
Shh who?
Shh yourself. I'm trying
to watch a movie!

Who's there?
Justice
Justice who?
Justice once, let me in,
please.

What do you get when dinosaurs crash their cars?

Tyrannosaurus wrecks.

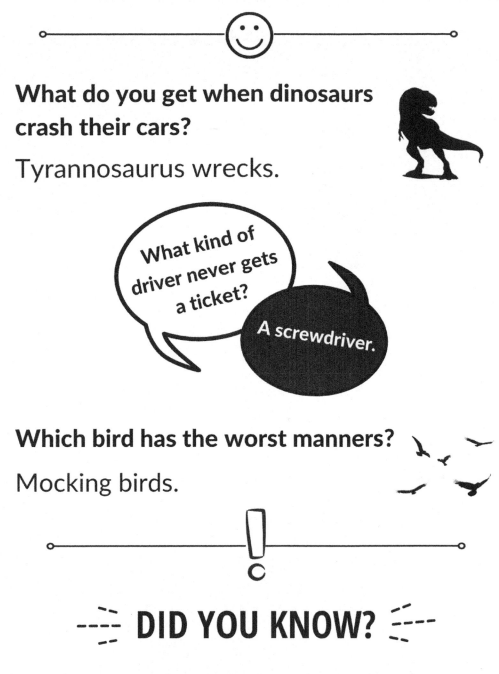

What kind of driver never gets a ticket?

A screwdriver.

Which bird has the worst manners?

Mocking birds.

DID YOU KNOW?

Until the 1970s and before alarm clocks became a thing, there were "Knocker Uppers" who would wake people up for work.

DID YOU KNOW?

The first person to go over Niagara Falls in a barrel and survive was a 63 year old female schoolteacher.

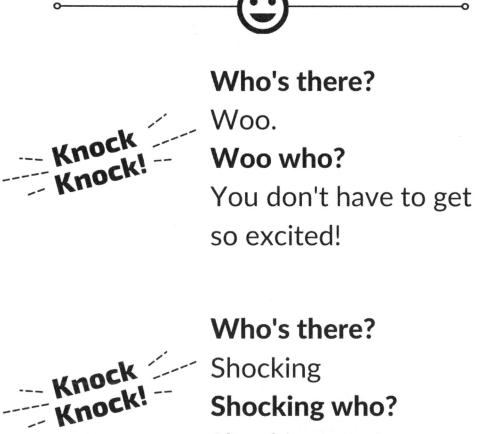

Knock Knock!

Who's there?
Woo.
Woo who?
You don't have to get so excited!

Knock Knock!

Who's there?
Shocking
Shocking who?
Shocking you!

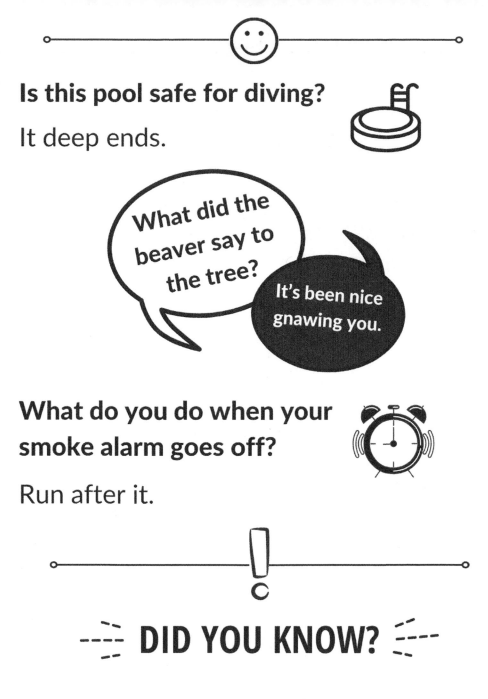

Is this pool safe for diving?

It deep ends.

What did the beaver say to the tree?

It's been nice gnawing you.

What do you do when your smoke alarm goes off?

Run after it.

DID YOU KNOW?

Grapes are fatally toxic to cats and dogs.

There are 3,160 tons of water that flow over Niagara Falls every second.

**Yally Bally had
a jolly golliwog.
Feeling folly, Yally Bally
Bought his jolly golli' a
dollie made of holly!**

TONGUE TWISTER

Who's there?

Ivan.

Ivan who?

Ivan to give you
a big hug.

Who's there?

Dwayne.

Dwayne who?

Dwayne the sink.
I need to use it!

Bob, I think you grew a foot over the summer!

I only got two!

What sort of appliance does a monkey use?

A gorilla. (A griller)

Why is a snake so lucky?

You can't pull its legs!

--⫶ DID YOU KNOW? ⫶--

There is an uninhabited island known as Pig Beach, located in the Bahamas, that is populated by pigs. They swim too!

**Salty broccoli,
salty broccoli, salty broccoli**

**Nothing is worth
thousands of deaths.**

Who's there?

Canoe.

Canoe who?

Canoe help me get inside?

Who's there?

Al.

Al who?

Al give you a hug if you
open this door!

What game do crocodiles like the most?

Snap!

When does a joke become a "dad" joke?

When the punch line is a parent.

How do you make a lemon drop?

Just let it fall.

A father's child, a mother's child, yet no one's son. Who am I?

The daughter.

RIDDLES

Some people like me some people don't. I can be good, but bad sometimes too. Who am I?

You.

What is worse than raining cats and dogs?
Hailing taxis!

 **How much does it cost a pirate to get his ears pierced?**

About a buck an ear.

 **Who's there?**
You Know.
You Know who?
Exactly. Avada Kedavra, Muggle!

 **Who's there?**
Jess.
Jess who?
Jess cut the talking and let me in.

Where would you find an elephant?

The same place you lost her!

The past, present and future walked into a bar.

It was tense.

What did Mama cow say to Baby cow?

It's pasture bedtime.

Knock Knock!

Who's there?
Hedda.
Hedda who?
Hedda feeling you wouldn't open the door.

I'm a sheet slitter.
I slit sheets.
I'm the sleekest sheet slitter
that ever slit sheets.

Railroad Crossing, look out for the cars. Can you spell that, without any R's?

That.

On which side of a church is the graveyard always situated?

On the outside, of course.

What sound do you hear when a cow breaks the sound barrier?

Cowboom!

What did the flower say after it told a joke?

I was just pollen your leg.

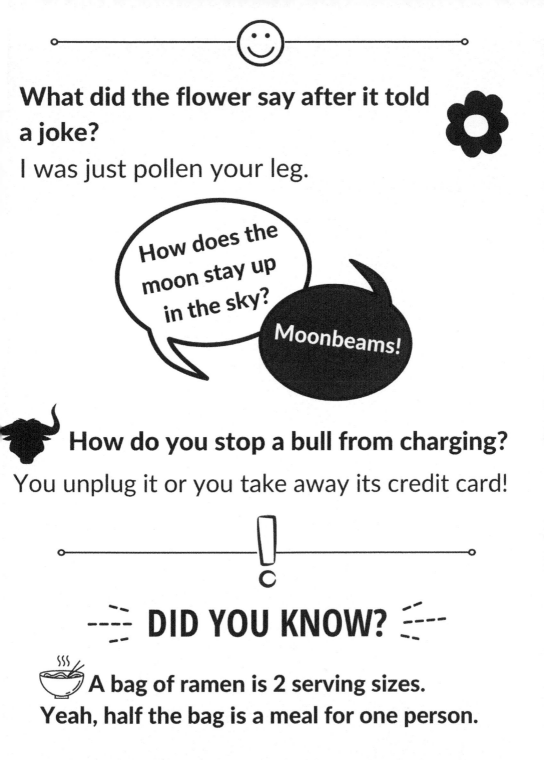

How do you stop a bull from charging?

You unplug it or you take away its credit card!

--- **DID YOU KNOW?** ---

A bag of ramen is 2 serving sizes.
Yeah, half the bag is a meal for one person.

Albert Einstein and Charles Darwin both married their cousins.

**A dragon will come and
beat his drum
Ra-ta-ta-ta-ta-ta-ta-ta-too
at a minute
or two to two today.**

Who's there?
Zipper.
Zipper who?
Zip-person standing
at the door.

Who's there?
Rena.
Rena who?
Rena this bell doesn't
do any good!

What did the dad say to his daughter at the cookout?

This grill is on fire!

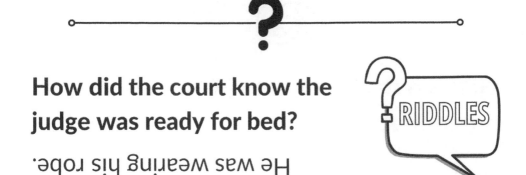

How did the court know the judge was ready for bed?

He was wearing his robe.

Why are trees in winter like troublesome visitors?

Because it's a long time before they leave.

Who's there?
Pammy.
Pammy who?
Pammy the key,
the door is locked!

Who's there?

Pepsi.
Pepsi who?
Pepsi through the keyhole.

What is a pirate's favorite body part?

The booty!

What do you call a pounding headache?

A temple tantrum!

What is the strongest kind of shoe?

Under Armor!

DID YOU KNOW?

Approximately 10-20% of U.S. power outages are caused by squirrels.

Knock Knock!

Who's there?
Yo
Yo who?
Yo mama!

Knock Knock!

Who's there?
Spain.
Spain who?
Spain to have to keep knocking on this door!

DID YOU KNOW?

Judge Judy is the highest-paid TV host.

You can find mountains and volcanoes on the bottom of oceans.

Leave Your Feedback on Amazon

Please think about leaving some feedback via a review on Amazon. It may only take a moment, but it really does mean the world for small businesses like mine.

Even if you did not enjoy this title, please let us know the reason(s) in your review so that we may improve this title and serve you better.

From the Publisher

Hayden Fox's mission is to create premium content for children that will help them expand their vocabulary, grow their imaginations, gain confidence, and share tons of laughs along the way.

Without you, however, this would not be possible, so we sincerely thank you for your purchase and for supporting our company mission.

Check out our other books!

For more, visit our Amazon store at:
amazon.com/author/haydenfox